KINDLE MARKETING VICTORY

Discover How To Market Your Kindle EBooks Successfully

Dominic. B. Frost

Dominicbfrost.com

Kindle Marketing Victory   Dominic. B. Frost

Copyright © 2018 Dominic. B. Frost
All rights reserved.
ISBN-13: 978-1986280310
ISBN-10: 1986280314

COPYRIGHT

February 2018 Edition
Copyright © 2018 by Dominic. B. Frost All rights reserved.

No part of this book may be reproduced in any form or by any electronic or mechanical means including information storage and retrieval systems except in the case of brief quotations in articles or reviews - without the permission in writing from its publisher, Dominic. B. Frost.

DISCLAIMER

All brand names and products names used in this book are trademarks, or trade names or their respective holders. I am not associated with any product or vendor in this book.

The information provided herein is stated to be truthful and consistent, in that any liability, in terms of inattention or otherwise, by any usage or abuse of any policies, processes, or direction contained within is the solitary and utter responsibility of the recipient reader.

Under no circumstances will and legal responsibility or blame be held against the publisher and author for any reparation, damages, or monetary loss due to the information herein, either directly or indirectly.

Please note the information contained within this document is for educational and entertainment purposes only. Every attempt has been made to provide accurate, up to date and reliable, complete information. No warranties of any kind are expressed or implied. Readers acknowledge that the author is no engaging in the rendering of legal financial, medical or professional advice.

By reading this document, the reader agrees that under no circumstance are we responsible for any losses, direct or indirect which are incurred as a result of the use of information contained within this document, including but not limited to, -errors, omissions or inaccuracies.

Kindle Marketing Victory   Dominic B. Frost

TABLE OF CONTENT

INTRODUCTION	1
WHAT YOU NEED TO DO BEFORE YOU MARKET YOUR KINDLE EBOOKS	2
MAKE SOME SMALL CHANGES WITHIN YOUR KINDLE EBOOKS	3
CREATE A GEO-TARGETING LINK FOR YOUR KINDLE EBOOKS	11
CREATE YOUR SOCIAL MEDIA ACCOUNTS	13
JOIN FORUMS	22
MAKE CHANGES TO YOUR WEBSITE	23
CREATE AN EMAIL NEWSLETTER	27
CREATE YOUR SOCIAL MEDIA CONTENT	32
FIND AND MAKE A LIST OF ALL THE KINDLE EBOOK REVIEWERS	42
BEGIN YOUR MARKETING CAMPAIGN	46
SETUP YOUR FREE KINDLE PROMOTION	47
SUBMIT YOUR FREE KINDLE EBOOK PROMOTIONAL DAYS TO FREE KINDLE PROMOTION WEBSITES	51
START YOUR SOCIAL MEDIA MARKETING CAMPAIGN	54
CREATE A FORUM SIGNATURE AND START POSTING ONTO FORUMS	70

REQUEST REVIEWS	73
HOW TO DEAL WITH BAD REVIEWS	76
OTHER MARKETING METHODS	79
WHAT TO DO WHEN YOUR FREE KINDLE PROMOTION BEGINS	88
WHAT TO DO WHEN YOUR FREE KINDLE PROMOTION ENDS	92
JOINT VENTURES	97
PAID ONLINE ADVERTISING	99
ADVERTISING AND MARKETING METHODS YOU SHOULD NOT USE	110
CONCLUSION	114

INTRODUCTION

Firstly I'd like to say thank you for buying my book.

I hope that with this book you will be able to market your Kindle eBooks effectively in order to increase the amount of readers and money you make.

You'll firstly be learning what you need to do before you market your Kindle eBooks.

You'll then learn about how to start your marketing campaign such as using the free kindle day promotion, submitting your social media content online and posting onto forums.

Finally you will learn about joint venture, paid online advertising and advertising/marketing methods you should never use.

I hope you enjoy reading my book and once again thank you for buying my book.

Dominic. B. Frost

Dominicbfrost.com

Facebook: https://www.facebook.com/Dominic-B-Frost-1486663614766022/

Twitter: https://twitter.com/DominicBFrost

WHAT YOU NEED TO DO BEFORE YOU MARKET YOUR KINDLE EBOOKS

Within the next seven chapters I will be explaining what you need to do before you start market your Kindle eBooks.

If you do not take these steps before marketing your Kindle eBooks them you will not be able to market your Kindle eBooks as effectively as you can which will result in less Kindle eBook readers, sales and money.

So please read the next seven chapters carefully before you market your Kindle eBooks.

MAKE SOME SMALL CHANGES WITHIN YOUR KINDLE EBOOKS

You should make some small changes within your Kindle eBooks in order to market your website and the other Kindle eBooks you've published.

By doing this you will increase the amount of traffic to your website and sales you'll receive from your Kindle eBooks and the other products/services you're either selling or promoting on your website.

What sort of changes can I make to my Kindle EBooks?

The types of changes you can make to your Kindle are as follows.

- Ask your readers to review your Kindle eBooks on Amazon.
- Ask your readers to connect to your social media accounts.
- Add links to some of the other Kindle eBooks you've published.
- Add your website links.
- Add your website sub domain links.

Ask Your Readers to Review Your Kindle EBooks

The more five star Kindle eBook reviews you have the more than likely people are going to want to buy your Kindle eBooks which will increase your sales/readers and your Kindle eBook sales rating.

This is because people will usually read your Kindle eBooks reviews before they decide whether or not they want to buy/read your Kindle eBooks.

If you have a lot of five star reviews then this will increase their confidence that they will benefit from reading/buying your Kindle eBooks which will increase your Kindle eBook sales and the more sales you have the higher your Kindle eBook sales rating will be.

This is why you should ask every Kindle eBook reader to review your Kindle eBooks.

Where Should I Ask My Readers To Review My Kindle EBooks?

You should ask your reader for a review either within the Conclusion, Thank You, Afterword or Author Note Chapters at the end of your Kindle eBooks.

How Should I Ask My Readers To Review My Kindle EBooks?

The message can be as simple as "if you enjoyed reading my eBook then can I ask you to write a favour and write a short review on Amazon" or "click here to leave a review of my Kindle eBook on Amazon" you should also add a link to your Kindle eBook web page.

How Can I Add My Kindle EBook Web Page Links Within My Kindle EBooks?

You'll firstly need to edit your Kindle eBooks so that you can add the link to your Kindle eBook web page.

You'll then need to re-upload your Kindle eBook by selecting the edit eBook content link.

Then once uploaded your new Kindle eBook will then replace the old Kindle eBook within the next twelve to seventy two hours.

Should I Add Links To My Kindle EBook Web Page?

By adding a link to your Kindle eBook web page you will be making it easier and more convenient for your readers to review your Kindle eBooks.

However adding the links within your Kindle eBooks is not essential as most readers will know where to go to review your Kindle eBooks.

Is There A Downside To Asking My Readers To Review My Kindle EBooks?

If your Kindle eBooks are rubbish and a lot of your readers wish they never read it then you'll receive a lot more one star bad reviews as you've made reviewing your Kindle eBooks a lot easier for your readers and bad reviews can decrease the amount of readers and buyers you will receive.

So the best thing to do is make sure your Kindle eBooks are really good before uploading.

Ask Your Readers to Connect To Your Social Media Accounts

When you have created your social media accounts (which I'll go over with you in the Create Your <u>Social Media Accounts</u> chapter) you should ask your readers to connect to them.

This will allow you to market any new Kindle eBooks you've published which will increase your Kindle eBook sales and readers.

You'll also be able to market your website and other products/services you are either selling or promoting.

Where In /My Kindle EBooks Should I Ask My Readers To Connect To My Social Media

Account?

You should ask your readers to connect to your social media accounts in the Introduction chapter which should be within the first few chapters of you Kindle eBooks and within the Conclusion, Thank You, Afterword or Author Note Chapters located at the end of your Kindle eBooks.

What Social Media Accounts Should I Ask My Readers To Connect To?

It's essential that you ask your readers to connect with your Twitter, Facebook, Google plus and YouTube social media accounts.

You should also consider asking your readers to connect with any other social media accounts you may have created such as Pinterest Instagram and so on.

Add Links to Some of Your Other Kindle EBooks

By adding links within your Kindle eBooks to some of your other Kindle eBooks you've published you will be increasing the amount of readers and sales of your Kindle eBooks.

This is because your readers are likely to be interested in some of your other Kindle eBooks you've published and by adding a link to your other Kindle eBooks you're making it easier for them to buy and read them.

Where Should I Add The Links To My Other EBooks?

If you're publishing fictional Kindle eBooks then you should only add your Kindle eBook links within the Introduction, Conclusion, Thank You, Afterword, Author Note and Other Books chapters.

If however you're publishing non-fictional Kindle eBooks then you can also add your other Kindle eBook links within the main content so that your readers can learn more about the topics they're reading about.

For instance if you made a Kindle eBook about playing a guitar and another about joining a band then you may need to refer your readers back to the playing a guitar Kindle eBook you've published so that they can learn more.

Where Should The Other Books Chapter Be Added Within My Kindle EBooks?

The Other Books should be the very last chapter within your Kindle eBooks.

What Should Be Added Within The Other Books Chapter?

You should write a message which asks your reader to check out some of your other Kindle eBooks you've published.

You should also add your other Kindle eBook covers, links and a synopsis.

What Else Should I Do?

You'll need to keep on adding and updating your Other Books chapters so that your readers know about your recently published Kindle eBooks.

What Shouldn't I Do?

Do not add too many pages within the Other Books chapters as you do not want the majority of you Kindle eBooks to be filled with Kindle eBook covers and links to your other Kindle eBooks.

How Many Pages Should My Other Books Chapter Have?

I recommend you should add no more than eight pages within your Other Books chapter.

The first four pages should have your Kindle eBook covers, synopsis and Kindle eBook links to your new and most relevant Kindle eBooks you want to market.

The other four pages should only include the Kindle eBook title and links to the rest of your published Kindle eBooks.

Add Your Website Link

It's very important that you add your website links within your Kindle eBooks so that your readers can visit your website easily which will increase your website traffic , Kindle eBooks and other products/services you are selling or promoting on your website.

Where Within My Kindle EBooks Should I Add My Website Link?

You should add your website link within the beginning and end of your Kindle eBooks.

Add Your Subdomain Website Links

Adding your subdomain website links within your Kindle eBooks is a clever method you can use in order to get your reader to visit your website.

What Is A Subdomain Website Link?

A subdomain is a link to your website but it doesn't direct your readers to your homepage but another web page within your website where you'll be able provide your visitors with more information and advice.

It usually looks something like http://dominicbfrost.com/subdomain/.

Where Within My Kindle EBooks Should I Add Subdomain Website Links?

If you're publishing fictional Kindle eBooks then you can add your subdomain links within the, Introduction, Conclusion, Thank You, Afterword and Author Note chapters of your Kindle eBooks.

If however you're publishing non fictional Kindle eBooks then you can also add the subdomain within the main content of your Kindle eBooks where you'll be able provide your readers with more information about a certain topic.

For instance if you have a list of websites which will help your readers then you could add the list to your web page or blog post rather than within your Kindle eBooks and then place the subdomain link within the content of your Kindle eBooks for your readers to click onto.

It benefits your reader as websites tend to change over time due to websites deletion, change to website ownership and so on.

You also don't have to change your Kindle eBooks every time a list of websites or information changes on a regular basis.

How Many Subdomain Website Links Should I Add In Each Kindle EBook?

You do not want too many subdomain links within your Kindle eBooks as you want to provide your Kindle eBook readers with information and advice within your Kindle eBooks not from other sources on the internet

Adding too many subdomains can also annoy your readers.

So you should only have five subdomain links within each Kindle eBook if you're publishing fictional Kindle eBooks and twenty to thirty subdomain website links if you're publishing non fictional Kindle eBooks.

CREATE A GEO-TARGETING LINK FOR YOUR KINDLE EBOOKS

When you've published your Kindle eBooks you will need to create a geo-targeting link for each of your Kindle eBooks.

The reason why you'll need to do this is because your Kindle eBooks will have multiple web pages based on location and marketing all these web pages is not practical or easy to do.

However if you only create one geo-targeting link for each Kindle eBook you've published then anyone who clicks and opens your geo-targeting link will be redirected to your Kindle eBook web page based on where the visitor is located.

Which Is The Best Geo-Targeting Link Service To Use For My Kindle EBooks?

The best service to use in order to create a geo-targeting link for your Kindle eBooks is Booklinker as it's easy to use and is primarily used for Kindle eBooks available on Amazon.

There are also other services you can use which I have listed on my website at http://dominicbfrost.com/geo-targeting-link-services/.

What Shouldn't I Do With My Geo-Targeting Links?

If your intend to market your geo-targeting links outside of your website then you should not add your Amazon Associate affiliate tags within your geo-targeting links.

This is because Amazon Associates prefers you to keep your affiliate links within your website.

You could use one geo-targeting link service within your website which will have the Amazon Associate affiliate tags and another geo-targeting link service without your Amazon Associate affiliate tags for marketing your Kindle eBooks outside of your website.

Or you could use the Amazon OneLink service to market your Kindle eBooks and any other Amazon Associate affiliate products you're promoting within your website and use a geo-targeting link service without the Amazon Associate affiliate tags so that you can market your Kindle eBooks outside of your website.

This way you comply with the Amazon Associates program and you can market a geo-targeting links outside of your website.

Where Should I Market My Geo-Targeting Links?

I'll explain where you should and shouldn't market your geo-targeting links within the other chapters of my Kindle Marketing Victory book.

But you can market your geo-targeting links within your Kindle eBooks as long as you mention where they'll be redirected to and you add no Amazon Associate affiliate tags to your geo-targeting links.

CREATE YOUR SOCIAL MEDIA ACCOUNTS

Creating social media accounts is free, easily done and can be one of the best methods you can use to market your Kindle eBooks.

What Social Media Accounts Should I Create?

You should create the following social media accounts.

- Facebook
- YouTube
- Google plus
- Twitter

These are in my opinion the best social media account you can create and use in order to market your Kindle eBooks and website but you can also market your Kindle eBooks and websites at other social media sites such as Pinterest, Instagram and so on.

Facebook

Setting up an account with Facebook is easily done on all you have to do is enter your details on the Facebook homepage at https://www.Facebook.com/ and then your account is ready.

I also recommend you upload a profile picture.

If however like most people you already have a Facebook account then you will not need to create another one.

What Should I Do after I've Created a Facebook Account?

The next step is to join Facebook groups and create a Facebook page.

Join Facebook Groups

Facebook groups are where people can interact, post and discuss about interests, topics and to express their opinions.

There are also a lot of Facebook groups dedicated to marketing Kindle eBooks which you'll be using.

How Do I Find Facebook Groups To Join?

I've have a list of Facebook groups you can request to join on my website at http://dominicbfrost.com/facebook-groups-you-can-request-to-join/.

You can also type keywords related to the topic or genre of your Kindle eBooks within Facebooks search engine and then select the group tab.

How Do I Join Facebook Groups?

You'll need to select the request to join button within the Facebook group web page and wait until someone accepts your request.

However you should never request to join every Facebook group you find all at once as Facebook will suspend you from joining and posting to anymore Facebook groups for up to two weeks maybe more if necessary.

How Many Facebook Groups Should I Join In A Day?

I recommend you join twenty Facebook groups a day and space the joining of the Facebook groups throughout the day.

I also recommend you take a day off from joining these Facebook groups and you slightly increase the amount of Facebook groups you join when you begin joining them again.

So your timetable could look something like this.

Monday	Join twenty Facebook groups
Tuesday	Day Off
Wednesday	Join twenty five Facebook groups
Thursday	Day Off
Friday	Join thirty Facebook groups
Saturday	Day Off
Sunday	Join thirty Facebook groups

Finally you should join no more than fifty Facebook groups a day.

What Else Do You Recommend I Do With Facebook Groups?

You should focus on joining the Facebook groups first before posting onto them.

Are There Any Tools Which Can Help Me With My Facebook Group Tasks?

I have a list of tools which can help you with your Facebook group tasks at http://dominicbfrost.com/facebook-software/.

Create a Facebook Page

A Facebook page is similar to a website or blog where you can add information about your Kindle eBooks and any other products/services you are either selling or promoting.

How Do I Create A Facebook Page?

All you have to do is log into Facebook and select the create a page

link which is at
https://www.Facebook.com/pages/create/?ref_type=registration_form.

You'll then have the option of either clicking onto the artist, band or public figure tab or the Entertainment tab.

If you've selected the artist, band or public figure tab then you'll need to click onto the choose a category drop down menu and select the author option.

If however you've selected Entertainment tab then click onto the choose a category drop down menu and either select the Book or Book Series option.

You'll then need to give your Facebook page a name and select get started button.

Your Facebook Page will then be created where you'll need to upload a profile picture and a Facebook cover photo.

YouTube

YouTube is a social media website where people can upload videos, subscribe to video channels, like videos and even make comments.

Setting up a YouTube account is very easy all you need to do is create a Google account by visiting https://accounts.Google.com/SignUp?continue=https%3A%2F%2Fmyaccount.Google.com/intro and enter your details.

You can even create a new Gmail account however this is optional.

Once done you'll need to create a channel by visiting the following link provided https://www.youyube .com/channel_switcher you'll then need to select the create a new channel tab and give your channel a name.

Create a Google Plus Page

To create a Google plus page you'll need to do the following.

1. Log into your YouTube account.
2. Visit https://www.YouTube.com/account_advanced.
3. Click onto the connect with a Google plus page button
4. Click onto the choose a better name button.
5. Enter your Google plus page name.
6. Click the agree to terms button and select done.

Your new Google plus page is now created and connected to your YouTube channel which means that video you upload onto YouTube will automatically be added onto your Google plus page.

What Else Should I Do With My Google Plus Page?

You should add your profile picture and header images within your Google plus page by visiting https://plus.Google.com select the profile link and then select edit profile where you'll be able to customize and upload your avatar and header images.

Join Google Plus Communities

Google plus communities is very similar to joining Facebook groups.

However Google plus is unlikely to suspend/restrict your account by joining/posting onto too many Google plus communities.

But to be on the safe side you should only join a maximum of fifty Google plus communities a day and no more.

How Do I Find Google Plus Communities To Join?

Simply enter within the Google plus search engine the keyword related to your Kindle eBooks and select the communities tab and you'll have a list which you can join by selecting the join link.

I've also have a list of Google plus communities you can join on my website at http://dominicbfrost.com/google-plus-communities-you-can-join/.

Twitter

Twitter is one of the best social media tools you can use because you can connect your Twitter account with your other social media accounts such as YouTube and Facebook.

This means that every YouTube video you upload and every Facebook post you schedule on your Facebook page is automatically tweeted onto your Twitter account which will keep your Twitter account more active.

You can also use other third party tools to help you schedule tweets, send welcome tweets and unfollow inactive Twitter accounts.

Finally you can use Twitter to let your followers know about your Kindle eBooks and any other products/service you're either selling or marketing on your website.

How Do I Create A Twitter Account?

Firstly you need to visit https://Twitter.com/ and setup your account which basically means giving them your name, email address and so on.

You should also not follow anyone on Twitter at this stage as you are not ready to market your Kindle eBooks.

When you have setup your account you'll need to fill in your bio and add your website and Kindle eBook links.

You also should upload a profile picture and a header image which could be your logo or one of your Kindle eBook cover images.

How Many Twitter Accounts Can I Create?

You can create as many as you like but it'll be hard to manage all your Twitter account and you'll have to use a different email address for each Twitter account you create so I recommend you create a maximum of three accounts.

What Should I Do Once All My Twitter Accounts Have Been Created?

You should connect your Twitter account to the following social media accounts and third party tools.

Unfollowspy

Visit http://www.Unfollowspy.com/ and click the sign in to Twitter button and authenticate by signing into your Twitter account.

Statusbrew

Visit https://statusbrew.com/ and click the Get Started For Free button then click the sign up with Twitter button and then authenticate by signing into your Twitter account.

YouTube

Log into your YouTube account and visit https://www.YouTube.com/account_sharing you'll need to click onto the connect button then authenticate by signing into your Twitter account.

You'll also need to make sure all of the radio buttons below the Share your public activity to connected accounts text have a tick within them.

If they don't then click onto the radio buttons and a tick should appear.

Facebook

Visit https://www.Facebook.com/Twitter and log into Facebook.

You'll then need to select the Facebook page you want to connect your Twitter to.

Then you'll need to authenticate by signing into your Twitter account.

What Should I Do Once My Social Media Accounts And Third Party Tools Are Connected To Twitter?

Once all your social media accounts and third party tools are connected to Twitter then you should do nothing as you're not ready to market your Kindle eBooks, website and other products/services you're either selling or promoting on your website.

However when you are ready then you will be using them in the following way.

Unfollowspy

You'll use the Unfollowspy to unfollow Twitter accounts and send manual welcome tweets to your recent followers.

Statusbrew

You'll be using Statusbrew to send automatic tweets about your Kindle eBooks, website and other products/service your either selling or promoting onto Twitter.

YouTube

You'll be using YouTube to automatic tweet your video uploads and video likes.

Facebook

You'll be using Facebook to automatically post your Facebook page content onto Twitter.

Can I Connect My Twitter account to Google plus Page?

Unfortunately you can't connect your Twitter account to Google plus page at the moment but maybe in the future this facility will be available.

JOIN FORUMS

You'll need to join forums related to your Kindle eBooks so that you can market your Kindle eBooks more effectively.

How Do I Find Forums?

You should use Googles search engine and type keywords related to your Kindle eBooks with the word forum at the end.

You'll then need to visit each website listed and see whether it's a forum and look and decide whether you want to join the forum.

I also have a list of forums you can join on my website at http://dominicbfrost.com/forum-you-can-join/.

What Should I Do Once I've Joined All the Forums I've found?

You should add your details within the forum, read the rules and make sure you understand and comply with them.

MAKE CHANGES TO YOUR WEBSITE

You'll need to make some changes to your website in order to market your Kindle eBooks and any other products/service you're either selling or promoting on your website.

I do not have a website what should I do?

If you do not have a website to market your Kindle eBooks then you need to get one immediately by buying a domain name, web hosting.

You'll also need to use a platform such as WordPress which is easy to install, has a selection of free website templates and has a very simple interface which will allow you to add the necessary content onto your website.

I have a list of domain registrars you can use at http://dominicbfrost.com/domain-name-registration-services/ and a list of web hosting companies at http://dominicbfrost.com/web-hosting-services/.

What Sort Of Changes Will I Need To Make On My Website?

The changes you will need to make on your website are as follows.

Add Content to Your Website

You may have already added content onto your website but if you haven't then you need because if your website has no content then you might as well not have a website.

What Content Can I Add Within My Website?

The content you can add within your website is as follows

- Written material
- Images
- Video
- Audio
- Kindle EBook Links
- Affiliate Links
- Product links
- Advertising Links/Banner

And so on.

What Information Should I Provide On My Website?

Your website homepage should contain the most relevant up to date content about

- Your new Kindle eBooks.
- Your Kindle eBook giveaways.
- Your Kindle eBook countdown deals.
- Any other products/services you are selling or promoting.

You'll also need to create subdomain web pages which will explain more about you, why you have created your Kindle eBooks and any other useful information you want to provide.

Finally don't forget to add some of the subdomain links within your Kindle eBooks.

What Else Should I Look At Adding Onto My Website?

You will need to look at adding popular keywords within your website content as these keywords can get picked up by search engines which will increase the amount of traffic to your website.

The best way to find the best keywords to add within your website is to use the Google keyword planner tool at https://adwords.google.com/home/tools/keyword-planner/ and enter words related to your website and Kindle eBooks.

You'll then need to add the more popular keywords or phrases within your website content.

However do not add too many of the same popular keywords within your website or make the content irrelevant to your website as search engines will penalize you for this.

Add WordPress Plugins

If you've created a WordPress blog website then WordPress allows you to add plugins.

These WordPress plugins can be useful as they can drive traffic to your website, analyse the traffic coming in and out of your website and so on.

I have a list of WordPress plugins you can use on my website at http://dominicbfrost.com/wordpress-plugins-you-should-use-on-your-website/.

Add Social Media Buttons

The social media buttons will help your visitors connect to your social media accounts so that you can provide them with more up to date information about any new Kindle eBooks you've published or any new deals, free days, products/service you are selling and promoting on your website and so on.

You can also use social buttons so that your visitors can share your website content with others within their social media accounts which will drive even more traffic to your website.

I have a list of social media button tools you can use at

http://dominicbfrost.com/social-media-buttons-and-icon-tools/.

Add an Email Newsletter Sign up Form

Adding an email newsletter sign up form within your website is essential as it allows your website visitors to give you their name and address which you can use to market to them via email about your new Kindle eBooks, Kindle eBook promotions and any other products/services you're either selling or promoting on your website.

I have a list of popular autoresponders you can use to create email newsletter sign up form on my website at http://dominicbfrost.com/email-autoresponder-services/.

I'll also have more information about autoresponders within the next chapter.

CREATE AN EMAIL NEWSLETTER

Creating an email newsletter is one of the best ways to market your Kindle eBooks and any other products/services you are either selling or promoting on your website.

How Do I Create An Email Newsletter?

In order to create an email newsletter service you will need to sign up to an autoresponder service.

I have a list of autoresponder services you can join on my website at http://dominicbfrost.com/email-autoresponder-services/.

Once you've signed up to an autoresponder service you'll need to create the sign up forms, assign the website pages your visitors will land on and add the sign up form onto your website.

This will all explained within the autoresponder service you sign up to.

You'll also need to decide whether you want to use a single or double opt in email service.

What Is A Single/Double Opt In Email Service?

A single opt in email service only requires your website visitors to enters their name and email address within the sign up form on your website in order to subscribe to your email newsletter.

However a double opt in email service will also require your website visitors who've entered their name and email addresses within your sign up form to go to their email account and click on a link in order to subscribe to your email newsletter.

Which Opt In Service Will Give Me More Email Subscribers?

The single opt in service will give you more subscribers however you may end up with some incorrect/fake email addresses.

You can also end up with people entering email addresses which don't belong to them which can result in some of your sent email messages being flagged as spam.

What Happens If My Email Messages Are Flagged As Spam?

If your email messages are flagged as spam too often then your autoresponder account can be at risk of suspension or termination.

My Autoresponder Won't Allow Me To Use A Single Opt In Email Service?

Most autoresponders will not allow you to use a single opt in email service because of issues with fake email addresses and people entering email addresses which don't belong to them.

So unfortunately you'll have to stick with a double opt in email service.

Which Opt In Email Service Do You Recommend I Use?

I recommend you use the double opt in email service as it's safer and you'll know your email subscribers want to receive email messages from you.

What Else Can I Do To Convince My Website Visitors To Subscribe To My Email Newsletter?

You could offer an incentive such as a free eBook, video or information.

What Should I Do Once I've Setup the Autoresponder?

You need to create email messages to send your subscribers.

What Sort of Messages Should I Create and Send To My Subscribers

You should mainly focus on creating and sending emails about your Kindle eBooks and the products/services you are trying to sell or promote on your website.

However you should also create and send messages which provide useful information and advice to your subscribers.

How Many Email Messages Should I Create?

You should create ten follow up email messages which your subscribers will receive on a regular basis and ten broadcast messages which will be sent to your subscribers when you run a Kindle eBook promotion or when you've just released a new Kindle eBook.

You'll also need to keep creating email messages for your subscribers so that your email subscribers continually receive email messages about your Kindle eBooks and other products/service your either selling or promoting.

How Long Should The Email Messages Be?

I would suggest a few paragraphs long.

Can I Add The Kindle EBook Geo-Targeting Links Within My Email Messages?

You are allowed to add your Kindle eBook geo-targeting links as long as it's not attached with the Amazon Associates affiliate tags.

However it might be better to add a link within the email message to the web page you're using on your website to promote your Kindle eBooks as it will contain your affiliate links for them to click onto.

Can I Add Affiliate Links Within the Email Messages?

You need to make sure it's OK with the affiliate program you're using before sending your affiliate links via email.

However if you can't send affiliate links via email then you can always add a link within your email message to a web page you're using to promote the affiliate products/service which will have all the affiliate links for your email subscribers to click onto..

How Many Email Messages Should I Send To My Email Subscribers?

If you send too many email messages regularly then you will get a lot of people unsubscribing and even reporting your email message as spam.

However if you send too little email messages then they'll forget they even subscribed to your email newsletter and may again either unsubscribe or report your email as spam.

So when you first start out you should send one email every two to three days.

The only exception to this rule is when you're running a Kindle promotion in which you'll need to send about two to three emails a day letting your subscribers know about the Kindle promotion.

Eventually when your email list grows and you start to publish more and more Kindle eBooks you'll need to send at least one to two emails to your subscribers every day.

CREATE YOUR SOCIAL MEDIA CONTENT

You need to create the social media content which you'll be posting to all of your social media accounts when your Kindle eBook marketing campaign begins.

What Social Media Content Will I Need To Create?

The social media content you will need to create are as follows.

Twitter Welcome Tweets

Creating Twitter welcome tweets will increase the content you will be post onto your Twitter account and can increase the amount of website traffic to your Kindle eBook web pages and to your website.

How Long Should The Welcome Tweets Be?

Your welcome tweets need to be fewer than two hundred and fifty four characters long.

However you need to mention the Twitter users who are following you within your tweets and you need to add any relevant hashtags which will attract twitter users into reading your tweets.

So I recommend you create welcome tweets which are two hundred characters long.

What Should I Write Within My Welcome Tweets?

You'll need to thank your new followers for following you and you'll need to ask them to check out your new/free Amazon Kindle eBooks and add the non-affiliate geo-targeting link.

You can also ask them to visit your website or check out a

product/service you're either selling or promoting on your website.

What Hashtags Can I Add Within My Welcome Tweets?

I have a list of hashtags you can use on my website at http://dominicbfrost.com/hashtags-you-can-use-to-market-your-kindle-ebooks/.

You should also look at your tweets and see whether any words can be used as hashtags such as #Amazon, #Kindle #eBook and so on.

How Many Welcome Tweets Should I Create?

You should create five to ten tweets which need to be different from one another and you'll need to change the tweets over time so you that you can market some of your other Kindle eBooks and let your followers know about your free Kindle eBook days.

What Sort Of Website Links Can I Add Within My Welcome Tweets?

You can add your geo-targeted links without the affiliate tags when marketing your Kindle eBooks.

You can also add your website links.

Can I Add Affiliate Links Within My Welcome Tweets?

I wouldn't add affiliate links within your welcome tweets as Twitter users do not like affiliate links and it can also have a bad impact on your Twitter marketing campaign.

It's much better to add your website links promoting the affiliate product/service within your website.

Scheduled Tweets

Schedules tweets are different from welcome tweets because you won't be mentioning any Twitter users.

Instead you'll be using the tweets to let everyone know about your Kindle eBooks, website, products and services you're either selling or promoting on your website.

The scheduled tweets should have hashtags and should either contain a link to your website or the non-affiliate geo-targeting links to your Kindle eBooks.

Finally you should try and use two hundred and eighty characters within your scheduled tweets.

How Many Scheduled Tweets Should I Create?

You should create ten to twenty scheduled tweets which will be sent out two to three times a day.

You'll also need to keep creating and changing your scheduled tweets as time goes by so that you can keep marketing your new/free Kindle eBooks, your website and any products/services your either selling or promoting on your website.

Can I Add Affiliate Links Within My Scheduled Tweets?

Because you're not mentioning any Twitter users you can add affiliate links within your tweets without annoying your followers.

You should however check with the affiliate program you've signed up to first before you do this.

Facebook Page Messages

You'll need to create Facebook Page messages in order to keep your Facebook page active and drive traffic to your Facebook page.

What Should I Write Within My Facebook Page Messages?

You need to write messages which will market your Kindle eBooks, website and any other products/service you're either selling or promoting on your website.

How Long Should My Facebook Page Messages Be?

They should be no more than one paragraph long.

How Many Facebook Page Messages Should I Create?

You'll need to send at least one message a day so I'd create ten to twenty but eventually you'll need to create more when your marketing campaign begins.

What Sort Of Website Links Can I Add Within My Facebook Page Messages?

You should add the geo-targeted links without the affiliate tags when marketing your Kindle eBooks. You should also add your website links.

Can I Add Affiliate Links Within My Facebook Pages?

It depends on the affiliate program you use as most affiliate programs prefer you to keep your affiliate links within your website especially Amazon Associates.

However if you can add the affiliate links within your Facebook messages then by all means add them.

Facebook Groups Messages

Facebook groups are a great way to market your Kindle eBooks as there are a lot of people who will be interested in reading/buying the Kindle eBooks you've published within the Facebook groups you've joined up to.

Can I use Facebook Group Messages to Market My Website and Any Other Products/Services I'm Either Selling or Promoting?

It depends on the Facebook groups you've joined, the Facebook group rules and whether the affiliate program you've joined allows you to market their products/services in this way.

For instance you can post information and links about your website and other products you're either selling or promoting within a Facebook group you've joined if they have no rules in regards to advertising websites, products or service.

However you cannot post information and links to your website and other products you're either selling or marketing within a Facebook group which prohibits selling and advertising or you've joined an affiliate program which doesn't allow you to market their products in this way.

You'll also need to keep in mind the theme of the Facebook groups and see if it's compatible with your website and other products/services you're either selling or promoting because if it's not then your post is likely to be deleted and it could lead to you being removed from the Facebook group.

Should My Facebook Group Messages Market My Website and Any Other Products/Services I'm Either Selling or Promoting?

I've found that marketing Kindle eBooks within Facebook groups is much better than marketing website and other products/services because of the following reasons.

1. Your Kindle eBooks are mostly what people will want to read/buy within the Facebook groups you've joined.
2. Most people will not visit a website advertised on Facebook groups.
3. The other products/services you're either selling or promoting are unlikely to be bought from Facebook groups you've joined due to the price range which is likely to be higher than the cost of your Kindle eBooks.

You'll also be able to use your Kindle eBooks in order to get people to visit your website and look at the other products/services you're either selling or promoting.

However it's completely up to you how you want to market your website and other products/services you're either selling or promoting.

How Long Should My Facebook Group Messages Be?

They should be about a paragraph long with links to your Kindle eBooks.

Should I Include Geo-Targeting Link Within The Facebook Group Message?

Some groups allow you to do this but some don't so you should use the U.S., U.K. Canada and Australia original Kindle eBook links and the U.S. should be the first link to use within your message as this is where most visitors will either buy or download your Kindle eBooks from.

How Many Facebook Group Messages Should I Create?

You should create about ten messages which should be all different from one another which you'll need to change, adapt over time.

Google Plus Community Messages

Google plus communities is another great way to market your Kindle eBooks as most people within these Google plus communities you've joined will be interested in reading/buying Kindle eBooks.

However creating new Google plus community messages is unnecessary if you've created Facebook group messages as you can use the Facebook group messages you've created to post onto the Google plus communities.

But most Google plus communities you've joined will contain rules on what you can and cannot post very similar to Facebook groups

So you'll need to read the Google plus community rules before you start posting your messages onto them.

Can I create Google plus Community Messages to market my website and other products/services I'm either selling or promoting?

It depends on the Google plus communities you've joined, the Google plus community rules and whether the affiliate program you've joined allows you to market their products/services in this way.

Should I create Google plus Community Messages to market my website and other products/services I'm either selling or promoting?

I've found that marketing Kindle eBooks within Google plus communities is much better than marketing website and other products/services because of the following reasons.

1. Your Kindle eBooks are mostly what people will want to read/buy within the Google plus communities you've joined.
2. Most people will not visit a website advertised on Google plus communities.
3. The other products/services you're either selling or promoting are unlikely to be bought from Google plus communities you've joined due to the price range which is likely to be higher than the cost of your Kindle eBooks.

You'll also be able to use your Kindle eBooks in order to get people to visit your website and look at the other products/services you're either selling or promoting.

However it's completely up to you how you want to market your website and other products/services you're either selling or promoting.

Should I Include Geo-Targeting Links Within My Google Plus Community Messages?

Some Google plus communities allow you to do this some however some don't so I would use the U.S., U.K. Canada and Australia original Kindle eBook links if you can't add the geo-targeting link within your message.

Create Video's To Upload onto YouTube

The more video's you create and upload onto YouTube the more popular your YouTube channel becomes and the more traffic you can drive to your website and Kindle eBook web pages.

However it is recommends you upload one video a day in order to make your YouTube channel popular which is time consuming so I wouldn't focus on creating too many video's as part of your marketing campaign.

You could instead just create one video for your channel which can be a trailer for your new fictional Kindle eBook or can be a personal video letting your viewers know about the release of your new Kindle eBook.

You cannot however create an advertisement for your Kindle eBooks as this is against YouTube policy.

How Can I Create A Video For My YouTube Channel?

There are many ways you can create a YouTube video however the easiest methods are as follows.

- Record the YouTube video yourself with a webcam or microphone.
- Hire someone to create the video for you.
- Convert one of your articles on your website into a video.

How Do I Convert One Of My Articles On My Website Into A Video?

I have listed a few tools available on my website at http://dominicbfrost.com/video-software-programs/ which will help you convert an article into a video.

What Should I Do When The YouTube Videos Have Been Created?

Once you've created your videos you should wait until your Kindle eBooks are published before uploading them onto YouTube.

However creating videos to market your Kindle eBooks is not essential.

FIND AND MAKE A LIST OF ALL THE KINDLE EBOOK REVIEWERS

You'll now need to find and make a list of all the Kindle eBook reviewers who may be interested in reading a Kindle eBook within your genre/topic.

Where Should I List the Kindle EBook Reviewers I've Found?

You should list the Kindle eBook reviewers you've found in either a text or spreadsheet file on your computer along with how you found them and the different methods you can use to contact them.

What Are The Methods I Can Use To Find Kindle EBook Reviewers?

Here are just some of the methods you can use to find reviewers.

Find Kindle EBook Reviewers on Amazon

To find Kindle eBook reviewers on Amazon you will need to do the following.

1. Type keywords related to your Kindle eBooks on Amazon.
2. Visit each Kindle eBook web page and scroll down to the review section.
3. Visit each reviewer web page on Amazon by clicking onto the name of each reviewer.
4. Look through their about section and see whether they have any social media accounts, websites and even an email to contact them with.
5. List their web page and contact methods within your text or spreadsheet file.

Find Kindle EBook Reviewers on YouTube

To find video reviewers to contact on YouTube you will have to do the following.

1. Visit YouTube and enter keywords related to your Kindle eBooks or type the following terms "eBook reviewers" or "reviewer".
2. Watch each video listed on YouTube, check to see if it's a good video with a lot of views and the check out how many subscribers the video channel has.
3. If your satisfied with the video and the amount of views and subscribers the channel has then you should visit the channel and select the about tab to see whether they have any other social media accounts, blogs websites you can use to contact them.
4. Check to see if they have an email address by selecting the view email address link.
5. Add all of the contact information within your text or spreadsheet file.

Find Kindle EBook Reviewers on Search Engines

You can find Kindle eBook reviewers on search engines by doing the following.

1. Visit a search engine such as Google and enter keywords related to your Kindle eBooks followed by Kindle eBook review, eBook reviews and other similar phrases.
2. Check out each website listed and see if they offer reviews.
3. Check their review policy and find out how you can contact them.
4. Add all of the contact information onto your text or spreadsheet file.

There is also a list of reviewers available at
http://www.theindieview.com/indie-reviewers/.

Find Kindle EBook Reviews On Forums

Look through the forums you've joined and look at the posts and check out people's profiles and see whether they've listed a website, social media or even their email address.

When you've done this you'll need to add all of the contact information onto your text or spreadsheet file.

Find Kindle EBook Reviews On Social Media Websites

You can search on Twitter, Facebook, Google plus and other social media websites by doing the following.

1. Enter keywords related to your Kindle eBooks within the social media search engine as well as phrases such as Kindle eBook Reviewer, eBook reviewers and other related keywords.
2. Looking through the search results and find out more from the listings about anyone who you can contact.
3. Add all of the contact information onto your text or spreadsheet file.

You should also avoid finding Kindle eBook reviewers within the Facebook groups and Google plus communities.

Why Should I Avoid Using Facebook Groups And Google Plus Communities To Find Kindle EBook Reviewers?

It might be tempting to find reviewers through Facebook groups and Google plus communities however you shouldn't because a lot of them may ask for Kindle eBook review swap.

What Is A Kindle EBook Review Swap?

A Kindle eBook review swap basically means that they'll review your Kindle eBooks as long as you review theirs which is against Amazons terms of service

I will explain what else you should and shouldn't do within the How To Deal With Bad Reviews and the Advertising And Marketing Methods You Should Not Use chapters.

BEGIN YOUR MARKETING CAMPAIGN

You will now be ready to start your marketing campaign after everything within the previous chapters of my book is setup correctly.

It may seem hard at first setting everything up but you'll find that it gets easier with the more Kindle eBooks you market.

For instance you do not need to create new social media accounts, join forums and create an email newsletter with every Kindle eBook you publish.

These accounts only need to be created once after which you can continue using them repeatedly with every Kindle eBook you publish and with every marketing campaign you run.

How Do I Begin My Marketing Campaign?

You will need to read the next few chapters in order to find out how to begin your marketing campaign.

SETUP YOUR FREE KINDLE PROMOTION

You'll firstly need to setup a free Kindle promotion which is an excellent promotional tool every Kindle eBook author and publisher should use.

What Is A Free Kindle Promotion?

A free Kindle promotion is where you will be able to give away your Kindle eBooks for five days within the 90 day KDP select enrolment after which you'll automatically be enrolled in the KDP select enrolment again and you'll be able to give away your Kindle eBooks for another five days.

Why Should I Give Away My Kindle EBooks For Five Days?

If this is the first time you've published your Kindle eBooks then you're unlikely to get any readers or sales because no one will know your Kindle eBooks even exist.

However if you give away some of your Kindle eBooks for free for just five days and you use the marketing methods within the next few chapters of my Kindle Marketing Victory book you will get people downloading and reading your Kindle eBooks which may lead to people buying and reading some of your other Kindle eBooks you've published.

How Will I Make Money If My Kindle EBooks Are Free?

If people read through your free Kindle eBooks and enjoy it then they're going to want to read more Kindle eBooks you've published and find out more about the author.

This is where you'll be able to make money as you'll have links within your Kindle eBooks to your website and other Kindle eBooks you're selling on Amazon which your reader are likely to click onto.

This will lead to an increase in Kindle eBook sales and an increase in sales of some of your other products/services you're either selling or marketing on your website.

You'll also increase your Kindle eBooks popularity which may lead to a few sales when it goes back on sale.

What Are The Other Benefits Of Running A Free Kindle Promotion?

You'll increase your website traffic, increase your email newsletter subscribers and increase the amount of followers within your social media accounts.

What Shouldn't I Do When Setting Up A Free Kindle Promotion?

You should never make all of your Kindle eBooks free on the same day because you'll lose potential sales and decrease the amount of money you'll earn if people download your entire Kindle eBook collection.

It's much better to give away your Kindle eBooks on different days.

You should also have your Kindle eBooks free for a maximum of two consecutive days, spread the free days over the next couple of weeks and make dates unpredictable so that people won't know if or when your Kindle eBooks will be free.

By doing this your free Kindle eBook rating will stay high rather than sliding back down, you'll increase the amount of Kindle eBook sales you make and you won't have people waiting until your Kindle eBooks are free again.

Finally you should not start your free Kindle eBook Promotions immediate.as some of the methods you can use to market your Kindle eBooks will require at least two weeks' notice and it will take time for you to build your social media following.

How Do I Setup A Free Kindle Promotion?

Here are the steps you need to take to setup a free Kindle promotion.

1. Sign into your Kindle account at https://kdp.Amazon.com.
2. Click and open the promote and advertise button next to the Kindle eBook you want to run the free Kindle days on.
3. Click onto the free Kindle promotion radio.
4. Click onto the Create a new free Kindle promotion button.
5. Select the start and end date you want to run your free Kindle days.
6. Click the save changes button.

You'll have to repeat steps 3 to 6 if you want to use multiple days which I recommend you do and you'll have to repeat steps 1 to 6 with every Kindle eBook you want to run a free promotion on.

Can I Setup A Kindle Countdown Promotion Instead?

If you've just published a new series of Kindle eBooks then I wouldn't run a Kindle countdown deal on your Kindle eBooks as it's highly unlikely anyone will buy your Kindle eBooks even if they're priced at $0.99.

You'll also only be able to run one Kindle countdown promotion and you'll be unable to run a free Kindle promotion until your next Kindle Select enrolment begins.

However if your Kindle eBooks are being bought regularly then running a Kindle countdown deal instead of a free Kindle promotion is a better route for you to take as people are keen to buy your Kindle eBook and decreasing the price will likely lead to an increase in Kindle eBook sales and profit.

SUBMIT YOUR FREE KINDLE EBOOK PROMOTIONAL DAYS TO FREE KINDLE PROMOTION WEBSITES

You'll now need to visit every free Kindle promotional website you can find and submit your free Kindle eBook days immediately.

I have a list of free Kindle eBook promotional websites at http://dominicbfrost.com/free-kindle-ebook-promotional-websites/.

You can also do a search on Google by typing "free Kindle promotional websites" or a similar search term.

What Will The Free Kindle EBook Promotional Websites Do?

When your Kindle eBooks are free they will list them on their website which will have a lot of website visitors all eager to download free Kindle eBooks.

They may even post your free Kindle eBooks onto their social media accounts, email subscribers and forums.

Will The Free Kindle EBook Promotional Websites Increase My Free Kindle EBook Downloads?

The free Kindle eBook promotional websites will significantly increase your free Kindle eBook downloads which may lead to an increase in sales of your other kindle eBooks and any other products/service you're either selling or promoting on your website.

How Much Notice Should I Give The Free Kindle EBook Promotional Websites?

You need to five the free Kindle eBook promotional websites at least two weeks' notice (maybe more in some cases) before your free Kindle eBook promotion will be listed within their websites.

What Else Do I Need To Do?

You'll need all your Kindle eBook details such as the title, sub title and so on.

You'll also need to go back onto their website and post your dates again if you have your free days scattered over a few weeks.

Do I Need To Pay To Submit My Free Kindle EBook Promotional Days To Free Kindle Promotion Websites?

Most of the free Kindle eBook promotional websites offer a free service.

However there are a few which will offer you more visibility on their websites and social media accounts if you pay.

Should I Pay To Submit My Free Kindle EBook Promotional Days To Free Kindle Promotion Websites?

If your starting out then no I wouldn't pay however it's completely up to you whether you want to or not.

Will All The Free Kindle Promotion Websites Market My Kindle EBooks?

Some free Kindle promotional websites have restrictions on what Kindle eBooks they will market.

For instance some free Kindle eBook promotional websites will only market Kindle eBooks if they're over a certain page length or a certain topic/genre and so on.

So you will need to read the submission policy within each free Kindle eBook promotional website before submitting your free Kindle eBook promotional dates so that you can be 100% sure that they will market your Kindle eBooks when your free Kindle promotion begins.

START YOUR SOCIAL MEDIA MARKETING CAMPAIGN

You'll now need to begin your social media marketing campaign in order to build up your social media following and market your Kindle eBooks and website effectively.

To do this you will need to do the following within each social media account you've joined.

Post Your Pre Made Messages onto the Facebook Group You've Joined.

You will need to stop joining Facebook groups immediately and start posting your pre made messages onto the Facebook group you've joined.

How Many Facebook Groups Should I Post In A Day?

You should not post your pre made messages to all the Facebook groups you've joined to immediately as Facebook will suspend you from posting onto the Facebook groups for two weeks or more.

Instead I recommend use the same timetable you used to join the Facebook groups.

So you'll post your pre made message to twenty Facebook groups a day and space the posting of your pre made messages throughout the day.

Then you should take a day off from posting onto Facebook groups and when you begin again you should increase the amount pre made messages you post.

Here is another example of the timetable you can use

Monday	Post your pre made messages to twenty Facebook groups
Tuesday	Day Off
Wednesday	Post your pre made messages to twenty five Facebook groups
Thursday	Day Off
Friday	Post your pre made messages to thirty Facebook groups
Saturday	Day Off
Sunday	Post your pre made messages to thirty Facebook groups

Finally you should post no more than fifty messages to Facebook groups a day.

Which Facebook Groups Should I Post My Messages To?

You should look at each Facebook group description and pinned posts to see what their rules are and before posting your messages.

If you find that your Kindle eBook and pre made message comply with the Facebook groups rules then by all means post your pre made messages onto the Facebook group.

If however you can't post your pre made messages because your Kindle eBook isn't running a free Kindle promotion just yet or your Kindle eBook isn't $0.99 or for any other reasons then you should move onto another Facebook group you can post to.

What happens if I break the Facebook Group rules?

If you break the Facebook group rules then your Facebook post will likely be deleted and you risk getting yourself kicked out of the Facebook group.

So always read and comply with the Facebook group rules before posting your pre made Facebook group messages.

Can I Post My Amazon Associates Affiliate Link within the Facebook Groups I've Joined?

Do not add any Amazon Associates affiliate links within the Facebook groups as this is against Amazon Associate terms of service.

Instead you should either use your original Kindle eBook links or the geo-targeting links without the affiliate tags.

Will I Need to Edit Some of My Pre Made Facebook Group Messages I've Created?

Yes you'll need to change some of your pre made Facebook group messages and create new ones as time goes by but this is all part of the Kindle eBook marketing process.

Post Your Pre Made Messages onto Your Facebook Page

You'll need to start posting your pre made Facebook messages onto your Facebook page.

To do this you should use your Facebook page scheduling tool by doing the following.

1. Sign into your Facebook account at https://www.Facebook.com/.
2. Visit Your Facebook page.
3. Click onto the publishing tools tab.
4. Click onto the scheduled posts link
5. Click onto the create button.
6. Either enter a new Scheduled Facebook post or copy and paste your pre made messages.
7. Click the schedule button.

8. Enter the date and time you want to publish your post and click onto the schedule button again.

By using the scheduling tool you can add all your pre made messages within your Facebook page within a single day and they can be posted over the next few weeks which will save you a lot of time.

Your Facebook page posts will also be tweeted if you've connected your Facebook page to your Twitter account which I recommend you do.

How Many Messages Should I Post Onto My Facebook Page Every Day?

You should schedule your posts so that one to two of your pre made messages are published onto your Facebook page every day.

Can I Post Affiliate Links Within My Facebook Page?

You should only use the geo-targeted links without the affiliate tags when posting message about your Kindle eBooks onto your Facebook pages so you don't break Amazon Associates terms of service.

However when it comes to the other affiliate programs available you should check to see if the affiliate program allows affiliate links within Facebook pages.

Alternatively you could write a Facebook page message promoting the affiliate product/service with a link to a web page within your website which will have more information about the affiliate product/service and all your affiliate links for your visitors to click onto.

This way you will be complying with the affiliate program rules, you'll be driving traffic to your website and you may make some money by promoting the affiliate product/service on your website.

Can I Repost The Same Facebook Page Messages After A Certain Period Of Time?

Yes you can repost the same messages within your Facebook page.

However you should also look at editing and adding new messages to post on your Facebook page.

Post Your Pre Made Messages onto the Google Plus Communities

Google plus communities is very similar to joining Facebook groups.

However Google plus is unlikely to suspend/restrict your account by posting your pre made messages onto too many Google plus communities.

But just to be on the safe side I would recommend that you post your pre made messages onto a maximum of fifty Google plus communities a day.

You should also use the same pre made messages from Facebook groups within Google plus communities as they're very similar to one another and you should check each Google plus Communities rules to see if you are allowed to post your pre made messages about your Kindle eBooks onto the Google plus communities.

Finally and most importantly you should never add your Amazon Associate links within your Google plus community posts.

Follow Twitter Accounts

Following Twitter accounts is by far the best way to gain followers because some of the Twitter accounts you've follow will likely follow you back.

Why do I need Twitter followers?

The more Twitter followers you have the more they'll likely read your welcome/scheduled tweets and click onto the links which will redirect them to either your Kindle eBook web page or your website.

This is why you need to gain as many followers onto your twitter account as you can.

How Do I Find And Follow Twitter Accounts?

In order to find Twitter accounts to follow you will need to do the following.

1. Type words such as Kindle eBooks, free Kindle and any other words related to your Kindle eBooks within the Twitter search engine.
2. Click onto either the latest or the people tabs.

If you click the latest tab you will find a list of Twitter accounts and their latest published tweets based on the keywords you've entered in the search engine.

In order to follow these Twitter accounts you'll need to hover your cursor over each Twitter account name and click onto the follow button.

If however you've click the people tab you'll have a list of Twitter accounts related to your keywords you entered into the search engine.

In order to follow these Twitter accounts you'll need to click onto each of the follow buttons within the web page.

You can also find more Twitter accounts to follow by visiting the Twitter accounts you've found and then by clicking onto either the followers or following tabs.

You'll then have a list of Twitter accounts you can follow by clicking onto each of the Twitter account follow buttons within the web page.

How Many Twitter Accounts Should I Follow A Day?

It's very easy to follow everyone you find on Twitter however if you do this you will end up being suspended for excessive following.

So you should start following a hundred Twitter accounts a day, space it out during the day and don't follow Twitter accounts too quickly otherwise Twitter will think your using a bot and will suspend your account.

You'll then eventually need to increase the amount of twitter account you follow as you'll also need to follow twitter accounts which follow you.

My Twitter Account Has Been Suspended What Should I Do?

This may have happen because you've either been following too many Twitter accounts or you've followed Twitter accounts too quickly.

However you can easily reinstate your Twitter account by giving Twitter your mobile number.

You'll then receive a text message with a number you'll need to enter within your Twitter account to reactivate your Twitter account.

However if your Twitter account repeatedly gets suspended then Twitter may make the decision to terminate your account.

So you should decrease the amount of Twitter accounts you follow and you should stop following Twitter accounts too quickly.

I Can't Follow More Than Five Thousand Twitter Accounts What Should I Do?

Twitter limits the amount of Twitter accounts you can follow to five thousand.

This limit will however be removed once you've gained more followers onto your Twitter account.

However once you are following over four thousand Twitter accounts you should start unfollowing Twitter accounts which have recently unfollowed you by doing the following.

1. Log into your Unfollowspy account.
2. Click onto the recent unfollowers tab.
3. Click the unfollow buttons within each Twitter account.

You should also unfollow the oldest Twitter accounts you've followed who are not following you back by doing the following.

1. Log into your Unfollowspy account.
2. Click onto the not followback tab.
3. Scroll down to end of the web page.
4. Select the last page within the jump to page drop down menu.
5. Click onto the unfollow buttons within each Twitter account.

Once you have over four and a half thousand followers or more on your Twitter account and the majority of Twitter accounts who are following you are also following you back then the limit should be removed and you can focus more on following more Twitter accounts rather than unfollowing them.

But if the ratio amount of Twitter accounts you're following is significantly higher than the amount of Twitter accounts following you then more following limits will be imposed on your Twitter account.

So I recommend that you regularly unfollow Twitter accounts that have stopped following you.

You can visit https://help.Twitter.com/en/rules-and-policies/Twitter-following-rules to find out more about Twitter following limits.

How Many Twitter Accounts Should I Unfollow In A Day?

Unfollowspy has a one hundred unfollow limit daily limit through there free service which you should try and keep.

However you may start to see your Twitter following numbers getting higher and higher so you'll eventually need to unfollow more Twitter accounts than the one hundred Unfollowspy limit.

To do this for free you'll need to do the following.

1. Click onto the Twitter accounts link within the Unfollowspy tool which will open the Twitter account holders' web page.
2. Hover your cursor over the following button within the Twitter account holders web page until the text changes to unfollow.
3. Click on the unfollow button.

Also to avoid your Twitter account being suspended you should do the following

- Avoid unfollowing too many Twitter accounts over the course of a day.
- Space the amount of Twitter accounts you unfollow over the course of a day.
- Avoid unfollowing Twitter accounts too quickly.

Should I Regularly Follow And Unfollow Twitter

Accounts On The Same Day?

When you're following over four thousand Twitter accounts you'll need to unfollow Twitter accounts one day, follow Twitter accounts the next day and then only follow Twitter accounts which are following you the day after.

Here is an example of a timetable you can use.

Monday
Unfollow one hundred Twitter accounts and only follow Twitter accounts which are following you.

Tuesday
Follow one hundred Twitter accounts and follow Twitter accounts which are following you.

Wednesday
Only follow Twitter accounts which are following you.

Thursday
Unfollow one hundred Twitter accounts and only follow Twitter accounts which are following you.

Friday
Follow one hundred Twitter accounts and Twitter accounts which are following you.

Saturday
Only follow Twitter accounts which are following you.

Sunday
Unfollow one hundred Twitter accounts and only follow Twitter accounts which are following you.

Will I Have To Keep Finding Twitter Accounts To Follow?

Eventually you will no longer need to find Twitter accounts to follow as they will find and follow you and all you will need to do is follow them back and unfollow Twitter accounts which are no longer following you.

When Should I Stop Finding Twitter Accounts To Follow?

When the five thousand Twitter account limit is removed and you start gaining regular Twitter followers onto your Twitter account.

Sending Welcome Tweets to Your Followers

Sending welcome tweets to your Twitter followers is a great way to market your Kindle eBooks and your website.

It also provides a lot of content on your Twitter account and it gets the attention of your recent followers.

However you will need to post your welcome tweets to your Twitter followers manually.

Isn't There An Automated Way I Can Send My Welcome Tweets To My Twitter Followers?

There used to be third party Twitter tools which would send automatic welcome tweets to all your new Twitter followers.

However Twitter recently decided to change its policy which prohibited automatic welcome tweets.

So unfortunately you will now have to send your welcome tweets manually.

Which Third Party Twitter Tool Do You Recommend I Use To Manually Send My

Welcome Tweets?

I recommend you use Unfollowspy to send your welcome tweets as the other do not have a manual welcome tweet facility available

How Do I Use Unfollowspy To Send Manual Welcome Tweets?

To send manual welcome tweets with the Unfollowspy tool you'll need to do the following.

1. Sign into Unfollowspy at http://www.Unfollowspy.com.
2. Click onto the mention tab.
3. Find the Twitter accounts you want to mention within your tweet and click the add to tweet button.
4. Either create a new welcome tweet or copy and paste one of your pre made welcome tweet within the text box.
5. Click the enter custom text button.
6. Click the tweet button.

Do I Have To Use The Unfollowspy Tool To Manually Send Welcome Tweets To My Recent Twitter Followers?

You can technically send your welcome tweets without using any of the third party Twitter tools.

However it will be difficult keeping track of your new followers and unfollowers which is why I recommend you use the Unfollowspy tool.

How Many Welcome Tweets Should I Post In A Day?

You shouldn't go overboard and send too many welcome tweets to every Twitter account that follows you as Twitter will think you're using a bot and will suspend your account.

So I recommend you send a maximum of twenty to thirty welcome tweets a day and make sure you vary the welcome tweets.

The only exception to this rule is when you are running your free Kindle promotional days whereby you'll need to send a welcome tweet promoting your free Kindle eBooks to every new Twitter follower.

Finally you'll also need to edit and create new welcome tweets over time.

Can I Post My Geo-Targeting Links Within My Welcome Tweets?

You can post your geo-targeting links within your welcome tweets as long as the geo-targeting links are not connected to your Amazon Associate affiliate tags.

Can I Post Affiliate Links Within My Welcome Tweets?

I would highly discourage you from doing this as this will annoy Twitter account users and a lot of affiliate programs would rather you keep your affiliate links within your website.

It's much better to create a web page where you'll add the affiliate links and promote the affiliate product/service and market the web page onto Twitter.

This way you won't be annoying Twitter account users, you'll be complying with your affiliate program terms of service, you'll be driving traffic to your website and you may make some money promoting the affiliate products/services on your website.

Should I Keep Sending Welcome Tweets To My New Twitter Followers?

You should start phasing out the welcome tweets to your new Twitter followers and start to phase in more scheduled tweets when you've got around five to ten thousand followers

The reason for this is because your followers will now be more than likely read and click onto your regular scheduled tweets rather than your welcome tweets and creating and sending welcome tweets regularly is a lot more work than creating scheduled tweets.

Plus you can always return to sending welcome tweets if the result of not sending welcome tweets means less followers and traffic to your Kindle eBook web pages and website.

Should I Bother Sending Welcome Tweets To My New Followers?

In my opinion it's a good idea to send welcome tweets to your new followers if you're just starting out and barely have any Twitter accounts following you as welcome tweets can do the following.

1. Provide more content on your Twitter account.
2. Increase the amount of Twitter followers to your Twitter account.
3. Increase the traffic to your Kindle eBook web pages and website.

However you should consider phasing out the welcome tweets after you've published a lot more Kindle eBooks and you gain a lot of Twitter followers on a daily basis as Twitter account users find them annoying and sending welcome tweets regularly is a lot more work than creating scheduled tweets.

Start Adding Your Scheduled Tweets within Statusbrew

You'll need to start adding your pre made Schedules Tweets onto

Statusbrew.

To do this you will need to do the following.

1. Sign into Statusbrew by visiting https://statusbrew.com/.
2. Click onto the publish icon.
3. Click onto the schedule link.
4. Click onto either the create button or the create new post button.
5. Click onto the choose profile link and click onto your Twitter account.
6. Either create a new scheduled tweet or copy and paste your pre made scheduled tweet within the text box provided.
7. You can also drag and drop images within the scheduled tweets.
8. Enter when you want your tweets to be published in the custom time section.
9. Click onto the save button.

How many scheduled tweets should be posted onto my Twitter account every day?

When you first start out you should schedule one to two tweets on your Twitter account a day.

However when you start to phase out the welcome tweets then I recommend you post ten to twenty scheduled tweets a day to keep your Twitter account more active.

Can I post my geo-targeting links within my scheduled tweets?

You can post your geo-targeting links within your scheduled tweets as long as the geo-targeting links are not connected to your Amazon Associate affiliate tags.

Can I Post Affiliate Links Within My Scheduled

Tweets?

You can add the affiliate links within your scheduled tweets if the affiliate program you've signed up to allows you to promote their products using Twitter.

If however the affiliate program doesn't allow you to market their products this way then you could always write a scheduled tweet promoting the affiliate product/service and add a link to a web page within your website which will give your visitors more information about the affiliate product/service and have all your affiliate links for your visitors to click onto.

This way you will be complying with the affiliate program rules, you'll be driving traffic to your website and you may make some money promoting the affiliate product/service on your website.

Can I Repost Scheduled Tweets After A Certain Period Of Time?

Yes you can repost the scheduled tweets within your Twitter account.

However you should also look at editing and adding new tweets to post onto your Twitter account.

CREATE A FORUM SIGNATURE AND START POSTING ONTO FORUMS

Posting onto the forums you've joined is an excellent way to market your Kindle eBooks.

However before you post anything you will need to create a signature.

What is a Forum Signature?

A forum signature is pre-formatted text, links and images which will appear automatically under each of your forum posts.

What should I add within the signature?

Within the signature you should add a little bit of information about you and your Kindle eBooks.

You should also check the forum rules to see what type of website links you can add within the signature.

Can I Add My Website Links Within The Forum Signature And Forum Posts?

You'll need to read the forum rules regarding adding links but a lot of them will not have a problem with it as long as you provide useful information within your website.

However if it's a forum about Kindle eBooks then I'd recommend you add links to your Kindle eBooks instead.

What Should I Do If The Forum States That I Can't

Add Short Links Within My Signature Or Anywhere Else Within The Forum?

If you can't add any short links within the forum then you'll be unable to add your geo-targeting links as they're technically short links.

So you'll need to post your U.S. and U.K. Kindle eBook links instead as this is where the majority of people will read and buy your Kindle eBooks will from.

Can I Add Affiliate Links Within the Forum Signature and Posts?

Most forums do not allow affiliate links anywhere within the forum and even if they do most affiliate programs do not like affiliate links being posted onto forums either.

So I would discourage you from posting any affiliate links within any forum you've joined.

What Should I Do If The Forum Rules States That I Cannot Add Any Links Within My Signature Or Anywhere Within The Forum?

If you can't add any links within your signature or anywhere else within the forum then you can still post information about your Kindle eBooks within the forum.

You can also mention within the forum that your Kindle eBooks are available to buy/download on Amazon.

By doing this you are not breaking the rules and you'll still be able to market your Kindle eBooks within the forum.

Some people within the forum may even search for your Kindle eBook titles on Amazon and take a look for themselves.

What Should I Do Once The Forum Signature Is Added?

Once the forum signature is added you'll need to find and open the Introduction or welcome thread and post a welcome message.

Make sure to also mention your Kindle eBooks and if possible add either your geo-targeting Kindle eBook links without the affiliate tags or the U.S. and U.K. Kindle eBook links.

You'll then need to regularly post information and advice onto the forums you've joined.

Finally you'll need to make sure that your forum signature appears automatically under each of your forum post for people to read and click onto.

How Many Forums Should I Post to and Interact with Every day?

You should only create new threads and post to around five to ten forums a day.

You should also check up on your old forums posts and see if you can post any more information, advice within the thread.

How Long Should I Spend Posting Onto Forums?

Try and limit the amount of time you post to forums to around an hour a day.

REQUEST REVIEWS

Requesting reviews is a great way to market your Kindle eBooks as the more good reviews you have the more likely people will want to read and buy your Kindle eBooks.

This will increase your Kindle eBook ratings which will increase visibility of your Kindle eBooks which can lead to even more Kindle eBook sales.

However there is no guarantee that the reviewers will give your Kindle eBooks a five stars review.

Some reviewers may even hate your Kindle eBooks and you'll end up with a one star bad review.

So you could be damaging your Kindle eBook ratings by inviting people to review your Kindle eBooks.

Should I Request Reviewers To Review My Kindle EBooks?

You should do one of the following first before you start asking every reviewer within your text or spreadsheet file to read and review your Kindle eBooks.

1. Wait And See What Your Readers Reviews Are Like First

Waiting to see what your readers reviews are like first before requesting reviews is the safest option as your reviews can easily be managed and any problems with your Kindle eBooks can easily be edited before you begin requesting reviews.

However one of the cons of doing this is you still might either get one or two bad review or you'll receive no reviews at all even after a few free Kindle eBook promotional runs .

If you do receive a few bad reviews then I recommend you read the How To Deal With Bad Reviews chapter.

If however you get no reviews at all then you have a choice of either carrying on without any reviews or you can use one of the other options available.

2. Ask Someone You Know To Read Your Kindle EBooks

If you are unsure whether or not your Kindle eBooks are any good and you want as many immediate reviews as you can then asking a few people you know to read through your Kindle eBooks is the best option for you.

However you should only ask people who will not be afraid to give you real criticism.

Which is why you should avoid asking close family and friends to review your Kindle eBooks as they're more likely to tell you what you want to hear and they may feel that telling you the truth may upset you.

There is also no guarantee that the rest of the reviewers will agree with their criticism so I'd look at moving onto the third option rather than asking every reviewer you have listed within the text, spreadsheet file to review your Kindle eBooks.

3. Ask A Small Proportion Of Reviewers To Review Your Kindle EBooks

Asking about five or ten reviewers to review your Kindle eBooks rather than the whole list of reviewers within your text or spreadsheet file is another option you can use as you'll not only be able to see how good or bad your Kindle eBooks are but you can also limit the damage if your Kindle eBook reviews are negative.

If you start getting negative reviews then you should read through the How to Deal with Bad Reviews chapter and look at asking another ten reviewers to review your Kindle eBooks.

Which Option Do You Recommend I Use?

It depends on how confident you are you've published a Kindle eBook people will want to read and how quickly you want people to review your Kindle eBooks.

For instance if this is your first Kindle eBook, you're unsure whether it'll get any good reviews and you're in no hurry to get a lot of instant reviews then I'd either wait until your readers review your Kindle eBook or ask someone you know to review your Kindle eBooks.

If however you're in a hurry to get as many reviews as you can and you are confident that your Kindle eBook is a masterpiece then you should ask a small proportion of reviewers to review your Kindle eBooks.

In my opinion however I think it's better to be safe than sorry and hold off on asking for reviews until your readers start reviewing your Kindle eBooks first and then consider asking your reviewers within your text or spreadsheet file to review your Kindle eBooks.

However whatever option you decide to choose is completely up to you.

HOW TO DEAL WITH BAD REVIEWS

If you've got one bad review out of ten good reviews for your Kindle eBooks then I wouldn't do anything as the good reviews exceed the bad reviews and nearly every Kindle eBook published gets one bad review.

But if you've got a lot of bad reviews and they're exceeding any good reviews you have then you need to read through the bad reviews carefully and find out what the problem is and decide whether your Kindle eBooks need editing.

How Do I Decide Whether Or Not My Kindle EBooks Needs Editing After A Lot Of Bad Reviews?

If you're still getting regular readers and sales of your Kindle eBooks then you shouldn't edit your Kindle eBooks at all as you're still making money from your Kindle eBooks and people still want read and buy your Kindle eBooks despite the bad reviews.

If however you're sales and readers are declining or you have no sales and readers due to the bad reviews then you'll either need to change the content of your Kindle eBooks or you'll need to delete the Kindle eBooks and start creating and publishing new Kindle eBooks within a different topic or genre.

What Should I Do Once I've Edited My Kindle EBooks to Address the Bad Reviews?

If you've made edits to your Kindle eBooks to address the bad reviews then try and see if you can contact your bad reviewers and ask them to read through your newly edited Kindle eBooks.

Hopefully this will convince them to either delete or change the review.

However never pressure them to leave you a good review, do not use threatening/abusive language in any way when contacting the reviewer and do not try and convince them to edit/remove their review in exchange for free gifts/money.

If you do any of these things when contacting a reviewer then you may end up having your Amazon account being either suspended or terminated due to violations of their terms of service.

It's better to be as polite as you can and only request that they read through your newly updated Kindle eBooks and see if they can edit their reviews.

What Should I Do If I Can't Contact The Reviewer?

If you can't contact the reviewer then you should move on and try to get more good reviews.

What Should I Do If The Reviewer Refuses To Change Their Bad Review?

If you reviewer refuses to change their review then you should again move on and try to get more good reviews.

A Kindle EBook Author Will Only Review My Kindle EBook If I Review One Of Theirs Should I Take Up The Offer?

This is called review swapping which you should never accept no matter how tempting it might be as it's against Amazons terms of service.

Why Is Review Swapping Against Amazons' Terms of Service?

The reason why review swaps are against Amazons terms of service is because no matter how bad you think the Kindle eBooks you've read is you will still give it a five star review because you want the author to give your Kindle eBook a five star review.

This means that the reviews you send and receive are not honest which is why Amazon has banned review swapping.

What Will Happen If I'm Caught Taking Part in a Review Swap?

If you're caught taking part in a review swap then it could lead your reviews being deleted, your Kindle eBooks being removed and in some cases further action can be taken against you.

So never take part in review swaps.

You should also read <u>Advertising And Marketing Methods You Should Not Use</u> chapter to learn more of the other marketing methods you should not use.

OTHER MARKETING METHODS

Some of the other marketing methods within this chapter will work but they will take a lot of time and work in order to implement and when it comes to your Kindle eBooks you need fast results.

However if you have some time available then I would recommend you use one or two of the methods within this chapter as it's a good idea to implement a long term marketing strategy in order to increase the amount of visitors to your website and Kindle eBook web page..

Create and Upload Video's onto YouTube Regularly

Creating videos and uploading them onto YouTube regularly in order to grow the popularity of your video channel is a lot of work and can be time consuming.

However there are tools which can help you create videos quickly on my website at http://dominicbfrost.com/video-software-programs/ and there are also tools which can help you automate some of the video marketing tasks on YouTube at http://dominicbfrost.com/youtube-marketing-software-programs/.

What Should I Do If I Intend to Upload Video's regularly onto YouTube?

When posting your video you shouldn't forget to post keyword tags, write a good title and description and include the links to your website, Kindle eBooks and other social media accounts you want people to connect with.

What Else Should I Do In Order To Market My Videos?

You'll need to look for video and video channels within your topic or genre and you should do the following.

1. Subscribe to their video channels.
2. Like their video's.
3. Post comments onto the video and video channel.

By doing this you will be marketing your video channel as people will visit your channel if you post comments on their videos, like their videos and subscribe to their YouTube channels.

You should also connect your Twitter account with YouTube so you will be automatically tweeting every time you upload and like a video on YouTube.

What Shouldn't I Do?

You shouldn't create and upload videos onto YouTube purely for advertising purposes.

So you'll have to provide content or information which will benefit your video viewers.

Is This A Good Long Term Marketing Strategy?

This is a very good method you can use to market your Kindle eBooks, website and products/services you are either selling or promoting on your website.

However this method does take up a lot of time and work which is why this is a long term marketing strategy which should only be implemented if you have the time to do so.

Create Unique Articles and Submit Them to Article Submission Websites

Creating unique article and submitting them to article submission websites may seem easy to do but you'll need to continually create and submit articles before you start to build any sort of traffic to your website.

Your articles will also need to be spelling and grammar checked and be over a certain amount of characters long so it's a lot of work for you to do especially whilst your creating Kindle eBooks.

What Do I Have To Do In Order To Submit My Unique Articles Onto Article Submission Websites?

You'll need to create a Title for your articles and a small resource/biography text where will give information about you, what you do and most importantly your website.

You then have to do the following.

1. Visit some of the article submission websites I've listed on my website at http://dominicbfrost.com/article-submission-websites/.
2. Sign up for a free article submission account.
3. Submit your unique article and resource/biography text to them.

They'll then publish your article on their website for people to read.

How Will Submitting My Unique Article To Article Submission Websites Help My Kindle EBook Marketing Efforts?

When a visitor reads your article they may decide to click onto your website link within the resource/biography section of your article.

You'll then be able to promote your Kindle eBooks and any other products/services your either selling or promoting on your website.

Your website search rating may also get a boost if it's a popular article submission website with a good search engine ranking.

What Am I Not Allowed To Post Within The Article Submission Websites?

You're not allowed to do the following

1. Post articles which aren't unique.
2. Post any website links within the articles.
3. Post your Kindle eBook web page links within your resource/biography text.
4. Post affiliate links within your resource/biography text.

You should also read the article submission websites terms of service to see what other rules and guidelines you will have to follow.

Is This A Good Long Term Marketing Strategy?

If you are just starting out then you are unlikely to get any traffic to your website.

However if you keep creating unique articles regularly then eventually you will start to see some traffic coming onto your website which can result in Kindle eBook sales and sales of any other products/services your either selling or promoting on your website.

But some of the other methods I've shown within this book are a lot easier to implement and can drive a lot more traffic to your website in a shorter amount of time which is why you shouldn't focus too much time and attention on this marketing method.

Guest Posting

Guest posting is basically creating and submitting a unique article to popular websites for them to publish.

It's very similar to the previous article submission method but it still take you a lot work in order to create the article and it can take months before you start to build any sort of traffic to your website.

How Do I Find Websites Who Will Publish My Unique Articles?

To find websites willing to publish your article you should do the following

1. Type your topic or genre keywords and either "write for us" or "guest post" in Googles search engine
2. Click on each website listed and see if they accept articles and content submissions.

What Should I Do Once I Found Websites Willing To Accept Guest Posts?

You should find out what there guidelines are and how you can submit your articles to them.

You'll then need to create and submit your articles to the guest post websites you've found which should also include your resource/biography text with your website links.

What Am I Not Allowed To Post Within Guest Posting Websites?

Every guest posting website has their own rules as to what they will/won't accept within your article.

However most guest post websites will not accept the following.

1. Article which aren't unique

2. Website links within the articles
3. Kindle eBook web page links
4. Affiliate links

Is Guest Posting Better Than Submitting My Unique Articles To Article Submission Websites?

Guest posting is a lot better than submitting your unique article to article submission websites because of the following reasons.

1. Guest post websites will have a lot more regular website traffic within the topic or genre you're writing about.
2. Guest post websites are likely to have less content than article submission websites which means your article is more than likely to be read by website visitors.
3. Your website page rating is likely to increase more if your articles are published on popular guest post websites rather than article submission website.

Is Guest Posting Harder Than Submitting My Unique Article To Article Submission Websites?

Guest posting is harder than submitting your unique article to article submission websites because these websites are likely to have a lot more restrictions.

It can also take a lot longer for these websites to publish your article and they're under no obligation to do so.

So you could end up waiting for weeks and in some cases months before you find out whether or not your article will be published onto their website.

Is This A Good Long Term Marketing Strategy?

This is a good long term strategy in marketing your Kindle eBooks, website and other products/services you are either selling or promoting on your website as the more articles published the more traffic will be driven to your website.

However your articles are unlikely to be posted onto the website immediately and even if they do it will take a lot of time before you start to see being driven onto your website.

But it's still a good long term marketing strategy which should only be implemented if you have the time to do so.

Create and Submit a Unique News Article to Press Release Websites

Creating a News article and submitting to press release websites is very similar to the previous article submission and guest posting marketing techniques.

However the big difference here is you are posting news worthy material.

This can be information about your new Kindle eBooks, new products or services you are either selling or promoting or it can be new developments on your websites.

It however isn't a place where you can provide advice for your readers.

I have a list of press release websites at http://dominicbfrost.com/press-release-websites/.

What Can I Add Within My News Articles?

You'll need to read and comply with press release websites terms of service before submitting your article

However I have found that the majority of press release websites will allow you to add the following within the content of your news article.

1. Geo-targeting Kindle eBook Links without Amazon Associate affiliate tag
2. Affiliate Links
3. Website Links

Can I Add Affiliate Links Within Press Release Websites?

You should check with the affiliate program you've signed up to first before posting affiliate links within your news articles.

What Shouldn't I Do?

You shouldn't add too many website links within your news article as this can put people off reading your news article.

Do I Need To Create A Resource/Biography Text With My Website Links?

You'll still need to create a resource/biography text as this will still be included at the end of every news article you submit your news article to.

Is This A Good Long Term Marketing Strategy?

This is a good long term strategy in marketing your Kindle eBooks, website and other products/services you are either selling or promoting on your website as the more news worthy articles published the more traffic will be driven to your website.

However it's very tricky creating news worthy articles and it will take a lot of time before you start to see traffic being driven onto your website if you decide to use this method.

But it's still a good long term marketing strategy which should only be implemented if you have the time to do so.

Offline Marketing

Offline marketing is basically marketing outside of the internet.

It can involve the following

- Handing out business cards
- Word of mouth
- Newspaper advertising
- Radio advertising
- And many more

All of the leaflets business cards and so on should have your website links and should also mention your Kindle eBooks and any other products/services your either selling or promoting on your website.

Is This A Good Marketing Strategy?

It depends on the offline marketing method you choose to use.

For instance handing out business cards and talking about your Kindle eBooks to your friends, family and associates is a good method to use as it's cheap and can yield good results.

However newspaper/radio advertising can be expensive.

You'll also find that some offline methods will have restrictions.

For instance you may need a permit if you intend to hand out leaflets in certain high streets.

It can also take a lot of money, time and work in order to get any website traffic using these methods which is why this is a long term strategy which you should only use if you have the time and resources available to market in this way.

WHAT TO DO WHEN YOUR FREE KINDLE PROMOTION BEGINS

When your free Kindle promotion begins you will firstly need to post on your website that you Kindle eBooks are free.

You'll then need to increase your marketing efforts of your free Kindle eBooks.

To do this you will need to do the following.

Facebook Groups

You'll firstly need to stop using Facebook groups to market your websites or other products/services your either selling or promoting so that you can dedicate your Facebook posts into marketing your free Kindle eBooks

You also need to increase your marketing efforts so that you can post to fifty groups a day without taking a day off in between days.

However you'll also need to avoid the two week suspension for posting onto too many Facebook groups.

So if this is your first Free Kindle Promotion and your Facebook account is new then you should only post to thirty groups a day without any days off in between.

You should then increase this amount of Facebook groups you post to when you're running another free Kindle promotion until you reach fifty Facebook groups a day without any days off in between.

Finally you should market how your Kindle eBooks will only be free for only one to two days within the Facebook group posts.

Facebook Pages

You'll need to double the amount of messages sent on the Facebook pages and you should only post messages marketing your free Kindle eBooks and use the geo-targeting Kindle eBook links within each post.

Google Plus Communities

You'll need to post to fifty Google plus communities throughout the day every day during your Kindle free promotion days and you should market how your Kindle eBooks will only be free for only one to two days within the Google plus communities.

Following and Unfollowing Twitter Accounts

You'll need to forget your daily scheduled planner and either double or triple the amount of followers you usually follow every day during your free Kindle promotion days.

You should also only unfollow Twitter accounts if Twitter will not allow you to follow any more Twitter accounts due to the following reasons.

1. You're following over five thousand Twitter followers.
2. Your following/follower ratio is unbalanced.
3. You've followed over a thousand Twitter followers in day (which you should never do).

Twitter Welcome Tweets

You'll need to use Unfollowspy to send your welcome tweets to every new follower you gain onto your Twitter account regularly.

You should also only tweet about your free Kindle eBooks and your tweets which should include your geo- targeting Kindle eBook link.

Twitter Scheduled Tweets

You need to double the amount of tweets you schedule when running your free Kindle promotional and you should only focus on marketing the free Kindle eBooks within your tweets.

Your tweets should also include your geo-targeting Kindle eBook links.

Forums

You need to post about your free Kindle eBooks within the free forum threads and wherever you can within the forums.

If you can't then change the signature and include that your Kindle eBooks are free for one or two days and post advice within the forums.

Email Newsletter Messages

If you have email newsletter subscribers then you'll need to send them two broadcast messages letting them know that one of your Kindle eBooks is free for the next one to two days

You should also include your geo-targeting Kindle eBook links within the email messages.

Reviewers

If you decided to request reviews of your Kindle eBooks then you'll need to send them letting know that your Kindle eBooks are now free to download.

What Will I Notice When I've Run My Free Kindle Promotion and Increase My Marketing Efforts?

You will firstly notice a huge increase in free Kindle eBook downloads.

You then may start to notice an increase in the following.

1. Website traffic
2. Email subscriptions
3. Social media following

This may lead to see an increase of some of your other Kindle eBooks sales and other products/services your either selling or promoting on your website.

WHAT TO DO WHEN YOUR FREE KINDLE PROMOTION ENDS

After your free Kindle promotion ends you should resume your normal marketing efforts and you'll need to plan your next free Kindle promotion.

What Else Do You Recommend I Do When The Free Kindle Promotion Ends?

You should keep creating and publish more Kindle eBooks.

Why Do I Need To Create And Publish More Kindle EBooks?

The more Kindle eBooks you create the more free Kindle promotions you can run.

You'll also be able to run an Amazon countdown deal with some of the Kindle you publish when they become more popular.

Will I Have To Run A Free Kindle Promotion With Every Kindle EBook I Publish?

You won't have to run a free kindle promotion with every Kindle eBook you publish because you will be regularly increasing your email list, your social media following and the traffic to your website.

This increase will mean that you can increase the popularity of your newly published Kindle eBooks without any need of a free Kindle promotion.

All you'll need to do is write a message about your newly published Kindle eBooks onto your website and let your email subscriber, social media following and forums know about your newly published Kindle eBooks.

Will This Mean After A Certain Period Of Time I Will Not Have To Run Any More Free Kindle Promotions?

You'll still need to run a few free Kindle promotions each month in order to gain new visitors to your website, increase your email list, and increase your social media following.

You'll also earn more money from your other Kindle eBooks you've published and the other products/ services you're either selling or promoting on your website by running regular free Kindle promotions.

Is There Any Way I Can Decrease The Kindle EBook Marketing Workload?

The amount of time and work you spend marketing your Kindle eBooks will eventually decrease.

This is because you will eventually not have to do the following.

- Find and follow Twitter accounts.
- Send welcome tweets.
- Join Facebook groups and Google plus communities.

You'll also be able to decrease the amount of free Kindle promotions you run and some of the other marketing tasks will become easier as time goes by.

Is There Any Way I Can Decrease The Kindle EBook Marketing Workload Further?

When you start making money from your Kindle eBooks you can

start looking at investing into some tools which will take some time off your hands.

For instance there is are tools listed on my website at http://dominicbfrost.com/facebook-software/ which will find and post to Facebook groups automatically in the way that you want.

There are also tools which I've listed on my website at http://dominicbfrost.com/google-plus-community-marketing-software/ which will do the same with Google plus communities.

You can also pay for a subscription to Unfollowspy which will get rid of the follow/unfollow limits.

Can I Hire Someone To Create My Marketing Content?

You can hire a virtual assistant who can do the following.

- Create Twitter schedule posts.
- Create the Facebook page posts.
- Create Facebook group and Google plus community posts.
- Create autoresponder email messages.
- Post your free Kindle eBook links to all of your free Kindle submission websites you've found.

However virtual assistants will cost money.

Should I Allow Virtual Assistants To Post My Marketing Content?

You should never allow a virtual assistant to post content onto your social media accounts, email subscribers or your website as they may start posting content which your website visitors, subscribers and followers dislike.

You should instead ask the virtual assistant to send you the content so that you can review it before publishing it online.

Can I Use Automated Tools To Post Onto Forums?

There are some automated forum software tools available which you can use to post onto forums.
However you should never use these automated forum software tools because of the following reasons.

- They're not very effective.
- They're mostly used to spam forums.
- The use of automated forum posts will likely result in you getting banned from the forums you've joined.

It's also tricky communicating with other people within forums using this type of software because each forum post and thread will be different from one another.

Can I Hire A Virtual Assistant To Post Onto Forums?

You shouldn't hire a virtual assistant to post onto the forums as they may start posting content which people within the forum dislike.

The best thing you can do in order to market onto forums is to create and post your own content manually.

I Want To Increase My Kindle EBook Sales Is There Any Way I Can Do This?

The next two chapters will show you how to increase your Kindle eBook sales.

However these methods should not be used until you have fully utilized the free marketing methods in your disposal and you're earning money from the sale of your Kindle eBooks and any other products/services your either selling or promoting on your website.

JOINT VENTURES

Joint ventures are a great way to increase the amount of sales to your Kindle eBooks and any other products/services you are selling on your website.

However you cannot start a joint venture until you have the following.

- Regular visitors to your website.
- A good social media following.
- A good list of email subscribers.

What's involved in a Joint Venture?

You will firstly need to find either a website owner or a Kindle eBook author within a similar non competing topic or genre

You'll then need to look at whether they have a similar amount of website traffic, social media following and email subscriber list compared to yours.

If they do then you'll need to contact them and offer them a deal whereby you'll promote and market their Kindle eBooks and/or products/services in exchange for them promoting and marketing your Kindle eBooks and/or products/services.

So I'm Basically Trading Marketing Campaigns?

That's exactly what you're doing which can yield great results.

Is This A Good Marketing Strategy?

Finding a Kindle eBook author or website owner to run a joint venture can take some time and you will get a lot of no's.

But when you have finally found someone who is willing to run a joint venture with you then you can both benefit from the deal.

PAID ONLINE ADVERTISING

Using paid online advertising to market your Kindle eBooks and website can significantly increase the amount of Kindle eBook readers, sales, website traffic and money you can earn from your website.

However you should use this marketing strategy with caution because it's very easy to misuse and overspend your money which could mean you'll end up losing money rather than making money.

This is why I recommend you should only spend money you can afford to lose when using this method.

What Should I Do Before I Invest My Money Into Paid Online Advertising?

You should firstly use the other methods within my Kindle Money Making Victory book in order to make some money from your Kindle eBooks and any other products/services your either selling or promoting on your website.

You should then consider investing around 25% to 50% of the money you have earned into the paid online advertising methods within this chapter.

Are There Any Other Ways I Can Spend My Money?

You could look at spending some of the money you've earned on Kindle eBook editors so that you can publish your Kindle eBooks more quickly you could also use some of the money to automate some of your previous marketing methods.

However using your money in this way is not essential.

What Are the Paid Online Advertising Methods I Can Use?

The paid online advertising methods you can use are as follow.

Advertise Your Kindle EBooks on Websites

Advertising your Kindle eBooks on websites primarily used to market Kindle eBooks is the best paid advertising method you can use to market your Kindle eBooks as the people visiting these websites are all Kindle eBook readers/buyers.

So advertising your Kindle eBooks on these websites will likely increase the amount of readers and sales of your Kindle eBooks.

How Do I Find Websites Offering To Advertise My Kindle EBooks?

You can search for websites that offer Kindle eBook advertising just by typing "Kindle eBook advertising" or a similar term on Google.

I also have a list of websites which you can use to advertise your Kindle eBooks at http://dominicbfrost.com/kindle-ebook-advertising-websites/.

What Should I Do Once I've found a Website That Can Advertise My Kindle EBooks?

You should firstly look at the website advertising page and see how many monthly visitors the website regularly receives and the amount of followers their social media accounts have.

You'll then need to find out how much they will charge either on a daily, weekly or monthly basis and how they will advertise your Kindle eBooks.

Finally you should whether there submission guidelines to be sure whether your Kindle eBooks complies with their rules otherwise they will not advertise your Kindle eBooks and they may even keep the money you paid them in advance.

What Should I Do When I've Decided to Spend My Money Advertising My Kindle EBooks within a Website?

You'll firstly need to your Kindle eBooks details to them.

You'll then need to test out how well their advertising works by limiting the advertising to just one day and see how many sales, downloads you get from advertising your Kindle eBooks on their websites.

What Should I Do If I'm Satisfied with the Advertising Test Results?

If you're happy with the advertising test results which have led to an increase in sales and downloads then you should consider advertising your Kindle eBooks on their websites on a weekly/monthly basis.

However you should never get carried away and spend too much of your money on advertising.

Make a daily, weekly and monthly advertising budget based on the amount of money your making from selling Kindle eBooks and any other products/service your either selling or promoting on your website and stick to it.

Buy Advertising space on websites

Buying advertising space on website is very similar to advertising your Kindle eBooks on Websites.

However you can also market your website or any other products/services you're either selling or promoting.

What Should I Do Before I Look For Websites Offering To Sell Web Space?

You need to create a promotional website banner which should be in a variety of banner sizes and resolutions.

How Do I Find Websites Who Are Selling Advertising Space?

You can find websites who are selling advertising space by typing your topic/genre keywords followed by "advertising" or a similar search term in Google.

What Should I Do Once I Found Websites Willing To Sell Advertising Space Within My Topic/Genre?

You should firstly look at the website advertising page and see how many monthly visitors the website regularly receives and you need to check out their social media accounts to see how many followers they have.

You'll then need to find out how much they will charge for the advertising space.

The Website Will Not Display How Much They Will Charge For Their Advertising Space What Should I Do?

They'll usually have an email address where you can contact them about what you want to advertise and how much they're willing to charge for the advertising space.

Once you have a price and it's within your advertising budget then you should try to haggle the price down further so you can get the best deal.

Will These Websites Advertise Via Social Media And Email?

It depends on the website that's offering advertising space however their likely to charge you more if you want to advertise this way.

What Should I Do If A Website I've Found Is Only Accepting A Minimum Of One Month Advertising On Their Website?

If a website you've found will only accept one month's advertising on their website then you could try and contact the website advertisers/owner and ask if you can advertise on their website for just a few days at a much lower price.

However if website owner/advertiser either does not reply or refuses your request then you should consider moving onto another website offering to sell advertising space.

Can I Add Affiliate Adverts Within The Website Advertising Space?

In my opinion it would be better to promote affiliate products/services from your website as some affiliate programs will not like the fact that you promoting their affiliate products/services in this way.

Also some website advertisers/owners are not going to like the fact that you adding affiliate adverts within their web space.

However if you want to promote an affiliate product in this way then you have to do the following.

1. Contact the website advertiser/owner and ask if they will allow affiliate adverts within their advertising space.
2. Look at the affiliate program you're using and see if they allow you to market their affiliate products/services this way.

If both the website advertiser/owner and the affiliate program have no problem with you advertising and promoting affiliate products/services in this way then you can add the affiliate adverts within their website advertising space.

What Should I Do When I've Decided to Spend My Money Advertising on Their Website?

You'll need to upload your website banner and enter your website details to the website owner/advertiser.

You'll then need to test out how well their advertising works by limiting the advertising to just a few days to see how much traffic you get on your website and how that converts into sales of your Kindle eBooks and other products/services you're either selling or promoting on your website.

What Should I Do If I'm Satisfied with the Advertising Test Results?

If you're happy with the advertising results then you should consider advertising your website on a weekly/monthly basis.

However you should never get carried away and spend too much of your money on advertising.

Make a daily, weekly and monthly advertising budget based on the amount of money your making from selling Kindle eBooks and any other products/service your either selling or promoting on your website and stick to it.

Pay per click advertising

Pay per click advertising is where you pay a fee every time someone clicks on your advert and visits your website.

It's a different model from paying on a daily, weekly and monthly basis as it guarantees people will visit your website.

What's The Best Pay per Click Advertiser?

The best pay per click advertiser to use is Google AdWords as they will put your advert and links within their search engine and will only display your advert and links when someone has entered keywords relevant to the keywords/ you've provided to Google.

I also have a list of other advertisers on my website at http://dominicbfrost.com/advertising-websites/.

What Should I Do Before I Create A Pay Per Click Advert?

You should either create the text or banner for your website advert.

You should also create a landing web page on your website where you will be marketing your Kindle eBooks or product/service you are either selling or promoting on your website.

What Else Should Be On The Landing Page?

The landing page should contain your email newsletter sign up form so that you can collect names and email addresses.

How Do I Create A Pay Per Click Advert?

Firstly you need to select an advertiser you want to use then you need to do the following.

1. Create either a text or banner advert for your website.
2. Provide them with keywords related to your website.
3. Provide them with your landing page website link.

The pay per click advertisers will also have instructions on how you can use their advertising service.

What Shouldn't I Do When Using Pay Per Click Adverts?

You cannot add affiliate links within pay per click advertising programs as most affiliate programs do not allow you to promote their products/services in this way.

Can I Directly Advertise My Kindle EBooks Within Pay Per Click Adverts?

You have to check with the pay per click advertisers to see if you are allowed to market your Kindle eBooks this way. but in my experience it's better to advertise your website landing web page rather than your Kindle eBooks as your website will be promoting all of your Kindle eBooks and other products/services.

What Is A Good Click Through Rate?

If after one hundred clicks you've sold either one of your Kindle eBooks or any other products/services your either selling or promoting on your website then you have a good click through rate.

If however you sold mothering even after one hundred clicks then you need to adjust the advert.

You also need to change your keywords or the pay per click rate if the cost of the pay per click adverts is more than the amount you've made from the sale of your Kindle eBooks or any other products/services you're either selling or promoting on your website rate.

Otherwise you will make a loss even if you've made a sale from your pay per click adverts.

What Else Should I Do?

You need to make a daily, weekly and monthly advertising budget based on the amount of money your making from selling Kindle eBooks and any other products/service your either selling or promoting on your website and stick to it.

Pay per Impression Advertising

Pay per impression advertising is similar to the pay per click advertising however the big difference is you do not pay per click but you pay every time a website visitor views your advert.

This in some cases can yield more results if you can pay less per impression and gain more clicks to your adverts.

What's The Best Pay per Impression Advertiser?

The best pay per impression media in my opinion is Facebook however I have a list of other advertisers at http://dominicbfrost.com/advertising-websites/.

How Do I Create A Pay Per Impression Adverts?

You would create a pay per impression advert in the same way you create a pay per click advert which is by selecting an advertiser you want to use for you pay per impression advert and then do the following

1. Create either a text or banner advert for your website.
2. Provide them with keywords related to your website.
3. Provide them with your landing page website link.

The pay per Impression advertisers will also have instructions on how you can use their advertising service.

Can I Add Affiliate Links Within Pay Per Impression Adverts?

You will need to check with the pay per impression advertisers and the affiliate program to see if you are allowed to market affiliate products/service in this way.

Can I Directly Advertise My Kindle EBooks Using Pay Per Impression Adverts?

You will again need to check with the pay per impression advertisers to see if you are allowed to market your Kindle eBooks this way.

However in my experience it's better to advertise your website landing page rather than your Kindle eBooks as your website will be promoting all of your Kindle eBooks and other products/services.

What Else Should I Do?

You need to make a daily, weekly and monthly advertising budget based on the amount of money your making from selling Kindle eBooks and any other products/service your either selling or promoting on your website and stick to it.

Other advertising methods

There are a lot more advertising methods such as video advertising pay per lead advertising and so on.

However before investing your money in any of them you will need to follow these golden rules.

1. Only spend money you can afford to lose.
2. Test out each advertising program first before fully investing in the advertising program.
3. Keep track of your daily, weekly and monthly advertising costs.
4. Keep track of how well your advertising campaigns are run and whether any changes need to be made.

ADVERTISING AND MARKETING METHODS YOU SHOULD NOT USE

The methods I will be showing you within this chapter should not be attempted as you will be damaging your marketing campaign, losing money, going against terms of service of some of the services you'll be using and you may even be breaking the law.

Buying, Swapping and Offering Incentives for Kindle EBook Reviews

You should never buy reviews for your Kindle eBooks as it's against Amazons terms of service which can result in your reviews being removed, your Kindle eBooks being removed and in some cases further action can be taken against you.

For instance Amazon has taken legal action against sellers buying reviews which you can read at https://techcrunch.com/2016/06/01/Amazon-sues-sellers-for-buying-fake-reviews/ and they've also taken action against fake reviewers which you can read at http://www.bbc.co.uk/news/technology-34565631.

Swapping reviews or offering incentives such as gifts is also against Amazons terms of service which can again result in your reviews being deleted, your Kindle eBooks being removed and further action can be taken against you.

Buying Social Media Likes, Followers, Subscribers and Video Views

You should never buy social media likes, followers, subscribers and video views because they're not real.

All the social media likes, followers, subscribers and video views are generated by bots which will not help you with your marketing campaign.

Using these services is also easily detectable by the social media websites you're using which can lead to termination of your social media accounts.

Buying Website Traffic and Backlinks

You should never buy website traffic as the sellers are either using bots to generate fake traffic to your website or the quality of the website traffic is poor and untargeted which will unlikely lead to an increase in sales of your Kindle eBooks or any other product/service on your website.

Buying website backlinks is also not worth doing as the majority of the backlinks will be posted on low quality websites which can damage your search engine rating and can result in less traffic being driven to your website.

You should also never buy these services to market your Kindle eBooks and affiliate products because it's against Amazons and most affiliate programs terms of service which can result in a termination of your Amazon/affiliate accounts.

Using Traffic Exchanges

What Is A Traffic Exchange?

A traffic exchange is a way in which you can gain website visitors to your website in exchange for you visiting websites within the traffic exchange network.

Why Shouldn't I Use Traffic Exchanges?

You should never use traffic exchanges because of the following reasons.

1. Some of the traffic isn't real and is being generated by bots.
2. The real traffic driven to your website by traffic exchanges will only visit you for a few short seconds after which they'll move onto another website they need to visit.
3. Some of the websites you will visit within the traffic exchanges can contain malicious content such as viruses, malware and so on.
4. Using Traffic exchanges to market adverts within your website is against most advertisers' terms of services.
5. Using Traffic exchange to market your Kindle eBooks is against Amazons terms of service.
6. Using Traffic exchange to market Affiliate products/service is against most affiliate programs terms of service.

Sending unsolicited marketing/advertising emails

Never ever send unsolicited marketing/advertising emails because it's not only against Amazon and most affiliate program terms of service but it's also illegal in most countries.

Please read the can spam act for more details at
https://en.wikipedia.org/wiki/Email_spam.

Does This Mean I Can't Send Marketing/Advertising Emails To The People Who Have Subscribed To My Email Newsletter?

You are allowed to send marketing/advertising emails to the people who have subscribed to your email newsletter \as they have opted into receiving these emails from you.

However if you continue to send them marketing/advertising emails after they have opted out of your email newsletter or your sending marketing/advertising emails to people who have never opted into your email newsletter then you are in violation of the can spam act.

What Else Is Not Against the Can Spam Act?

If you're emailing friends/family and businesses about an enquiry or arranging a meeting or anything professional/personal then this is not against the can spam act as you are not marketing/advertising any products/services.

Are There Any Other Reasons Why I Shouldn't Send Unsolicited Emails?

Sending unsolicited emails is not a very effective marketing/advertising strategy because of the following reasons.

1. Barely anyone receives the unsolicited email due to email filters.
2. Most unsolicited email will end up in the spam folder.
3. Barely anyone opens and reads the emails within the spam folder.

You could end up sending thousands upon thousands of emails and only get one person reading through your email so never ever send unsolicited marketing/advertising emails messages.

CONCLUSION

Marketing your Kindle eBooks takes a lot of time and work.

However it gets a lot easier as time goes by and with the more Kindle eBooks you publish and market regularly.

You may also start to see some money coming in which you can use for marketing and advertising purposes.

But you need to keep track of how much you spend to ensure you don't end up making a loss.

You'll also eventually reach a point where you find it hard to manage all of your Kindle eBooks and will need to know what to do when your Kindle eBook downloads and sales start decreasing.

Which is why I recommend you read my [Kindle Empire Management Victory](#) book which will show you what to do when these problems occurs.

THANK YOU

Finally I'd like to say thank you for buying my book.

If you enjoyed reading my book then I'd really appreciate it if you would post a short review on Amazon by visiting the link below.

https://www.amazon.com/dp/B07B7PBWD4

Also please check out my other Kindle and Paperback books available in the following pages and check out my websites at http://dominicbfrost.com/ for more information and updates.

Dominic. B. Frost

http://dominicbfrost.com/

Facebook: https://www.facebook.com/Dominic-B-Frost-1486663614766022/

Twitter: https://twitter.com/DominicBFrost

OTHER BOOKS

Available To Buy From Amazon At
 https://www.amazon.com/dp/B07B7NKS67
Get Your Copy Now

Available To Buy From Amazon At
https://www.amazon.com/dp/B07B7NX43W
Get Your Copy Now

Available To Buy From Amazon At
https://www.amazon.com/dp/B07B7PPYS2
Get Your Copy Now

www.ingramcontent.com/pod-product-compliance
Lightning Source LLC
Chambersburg PA
CBHW070147230526
45471CB00002B/550